JOHN TYLER

ENCYCLOPEDIA of PRESIDENTS

John Tyler

Tenth President of the United States

By Dee Lillegard

Consultant: Charles Abele, Ph.D.
Social Studies Instructor
Chicago Public School System

 CHILDRENS PRESS ®

CHICAGO

**John Tyler,
tenth president of
the United States**

For Collin Quincy, who shared the annexation of Texas with me

Library of Congress Cataloging-in-Publication Data

Lillegard, Dee.
  John Tyler.

  (Encyclopedia of presidents)
  Includes index.
  Summary: A biography of the Virginian who became
tenth president of the United States upon the death
of William Henry Harrison.
  1. Tyler, John, 1790-1862—Juvenile literature.
2. Presidents—United States—Biography—Juvenile
literature. [1. Tyler, John, 1790-1862. 2. Presidents]
I. Title. II. Series.
E397.L55   1987   973.5'8 [92]   87-18202
ISBN 0-516-01393-9

Picture Acknowledgments

The Bettmann Archive—4, 5, 6, 10, 19, 22
(2 photos), 43 (2 photos), 45, 46, 47, 48, 49, 50,
55, 58, 59, 60, 63, 65, 66, 68 (bottom), 69
(bottom), 72, 73, 77 (top), 79, 82, 86

Essex Institute/North Wind Pictures—76

Historical Pictures Service—8, 9, 11, 13, 26
(3 photos), 31, 32, 39, 41, 44, 51, 52, 57, 61
(bottom), 64, 68 (top), 74, 75, 77 (bottom), 78
(left), 80, 81, 83, 88, 89

Courtesy Library of Congress—30, 34, 35

Courtesy National Archives—27

North Wind Picture Archives—14, 18, 20, 24,
25 (2 photos), 29, 54, 61 (top), 70, 71, 78
(right)

Photri—40, 69 (top)

H. Armstrong Roberts—36

U.S. Bureau of Printing and Engraving—2, 23,
28

Cover design and illustration by
Steven Gaston Dobson

A "Hard Cider and Log Cabin" campaign poster for the 1840 presidential campaign, in which William Henry Harrison ran for president and John Tyler for vice-president

Table of Contents

HARRISONIAN

BALL ROLLING.

KEEP THE

WILLIAM HENRY HARRISON THE FARMER OF NORTH BEND.

RALLY!

A General Meeting

Will be held at the Old COURT ROOM, [Riey's building]

On Saturday Evening,

The 18th instant, at early candle light.   A punctual attendance is requested.

MESSRS. DAVIS, BOTKIN, KEATING

And others, will address the Meeting.

R. P. TODD, *Chairman*
Vigilance Committee.

July 17, 1840.

Chapter 1

"Honest John"

"Tippecanoe and Tyler, too!" That Whig slogan swept the country in the outlandish campaign of 1840. Wild rallies and parades sprang up everywhere as boisterous Whigs rolled giant balls—ten or twelve feet wide—from state to state. The idea was to "Keep the ball rolling" for William Henry Harrison, all the way to Washington.

Harrison, the Whig presidential candidate, was the aging hero of Tippecanoe, a battle fought nearly thirty years earlier. His running mate, John Tyler, was a tall, thin southern gentleman. A Virginian and a former Democrat, Tyler had been chosen by the Whigs simply to draw southern votes. Nobody thought the office of vice-president was very important.

Although slavery had become a disturbing issue by 1840, the Whigs took no stand on this or any other issue. Instead, they campaigned with a flood of music and songs about Harrison, their military hero. They hoped this would keep northerners from thinking about slavery. With Tyler, they expected to win votes in the South.

Above: The inauguration of William Henry Harrison
Opposite page: A "Tippecanoe and Tyler, too" parade in Philadelphia

The Whig strategy worked. Harrison and Tyler won an overwhelming victory in the election. Some people said that Harrison had been "sung into the presidency." A Democratic editor complained: "Men, women and children did nothing but sing. It worried, annoyed, dumbfounded, crushed the Democrats, but there was no use trying to escape."

The Whigs got what they wanted; "Old Tippecanoe" was in the White House. But they were in for a sad surprise.

The death of William Henry Harrison on April 4, 1841

As soon as the inauguration of March 4, 1841, was over, John Tyler returned to his home in Williamsburg, Virginia. Expecting to play only a small role in the government of his country, he left the White House behind him. At dawn on April 5, a knock at his door roused the vice-president. Two messengers informed him that he must come to Washington at once. Harrison had died the day before of pneumonia—the first president of the United States to die in office.

Tyler receives word of President Harrison's death.

Tyler quickly prepared for the journey. He and his two grown sons traveled by horse, boat, and special train to the capital. It took them twenty-one hours to go from Williamsburg to Washington, D.C., a record for speed in 1841, though today a person can drive the same distance in less than three hours.

Once in Washington, Tyler established himself at Brown's Indian Queen Hotel. He immediately sent for Harrison's cabinet members, or advisers, who were the leaders of the Whig party.

The Constitution did not say exactly what should be done after the death of a president. The last surviving man who helped draw up the Constitution, James Madison, had died in 1836, and no one knew what he and the others at the Constitutional Convention had intended. Should the vice-president automatically become president? Or should he perform only certain presidential duties until another president could be elected?

The cabinet had already decided that Tyler should "bear the title of 'Vice-President, Acting President.'" Furthermore, Tyler was informed that he should do as Harrison had done before him—rely on the cabinet for all decisions relating to his administration.

John Tyler responded firmly to these instructions. "I can never consent to being dictated to," he said. "I, as President, shall be responsible for my administration."

The battle was on. The Whigs in Congress and in the cabinet were not about to let Tyler take over. For his part, Tyler made it clear that he was the president now, not merely an acting president.

Tyler had the courage to do what he believed was right. He took the oath of office as the tenth president of the United States, then infuriated the Whigs by vetoing the laws they passed.

When the cabinet tried to force him to resign, Tyler held his ground. "My resignation," he said, "would amount to a declaration to the world that our system of government had failed."

If he gave in to the Whig party, Tyler reasoned, the executive branch of the government (the presidency)

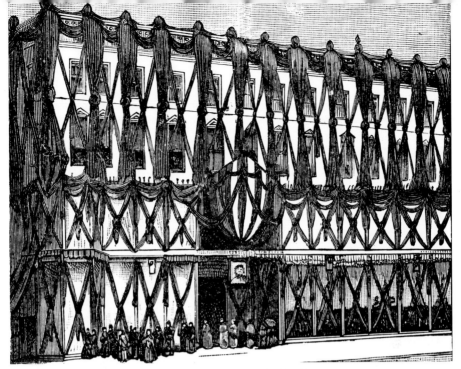

A building draped in mourning after Harrison's death

would lose its power to the legislative branch (Congress). This must not happen. The branches of the government, he felt, must maintain their delicate balance of power. Upon the death of a president, Tyler insisted, the vice-president must take the office with full power as the chief executive. This policy has remained in force to this day.

This issue was only the beginning of Tyler's battle with the Whigs. But no one should have been surprised at his single-mindedness. For years, Tyler had been known as "Honest John." A friend once said of him: "When he thinks he is right he is obstinate as a bull, and no power on earth can move him."

Calm, dignified, patient—John Tyler began an administration that he later called "a bed of thorns." He would become a president without a party. He would be burned in effigy by angry mobs, and Congress would try to impeach him. But John Tyler was made of strong stuff.

The Tyler residence at Greenway Plantation

Chapter 2

From Greenway
to Williamsburg

On March 29, 1790, John Tyler was born on his father's estate, called Greenway Plantation, in Charles City County, Virginia. This was the same county where William Henry Harrison had been born seventeen years earlier, though Harrison's name became associated with the West. Like Harrison, Tyler was the son of a southern planter who was also, for a time, the governor of Virginia.

When Tyler was born, George Washington had been president for one year. The first national census set the population of the United States at four million. About half the people who were counted lived in the South.

John Tyler was the first president of the United States to be born after the revolutionary war. He was the sixth child of Judge John Tyler and Mary Armistead Tyler. Judge Tyler served at various times as speaker of the Virginia House of Delegates and judge of the state and federal courts, as well as governor.

Judge Tyler was kind and well liked. During the course of his career, he became the guardian of twenty-one children. Along with his own eight, these children enlivened daily life at Greenway Plantation. Young John never lacked for the company of others.

Greenway, located on the James River, consisted of twelve hundred acres of fertile land. It was called Greenway because, as Tyler's oldest sister once said, "the grass grew so green there." The estate included a dairy, meathouse, granaries, and stables, plus servants' quarters and several houses for slaves. There was also an octagon-shaped pigeon house, well stocked with pigeons. Wheat, corn, and tobacco, as well as vegetable and flower gardens, thrived in Greenway's rich soil.

In front of the mansion stood a large willow tree. Beneath this willow, John and the other children often gathered to listen to Judge Tyler's stories about the revolutionary war or to hear him play the violin.

Mrs. Tyler took great pride in making her home and surroundings beautiful. She kept the front yard filled with roses, tulips, hyacinths, and lilies. When John was a baby, she is reported to have said, "This child is destined to be a President of the United States." She did not live to see her prophecy fulfilled; she died when John was only seven.

Mrs. Bagby, the old housekeeper who helped to raise John, described him as being gentle like his mother, with silky brown hair and bright blue eyes. As a boy, Tyler was generally mild mannered. Later, like his father, he would write poetry and play the violin. But there was another side to him.

Bright and headstrong, Tyler also inherited a fiery spirit from his father. When he was eleven, he led a rebellion of pupils against his tyrannical Scottish schoolmaster, William McMurdo. McMurdo's authority had never been questioned by the parents or guardians of his pupils. He was an intelligent man, well versed in his subjects; but he used birch switches from the swamp to whip his pupils mercilessly.

One day, under young John's leadership, the boys threw McMurdo down, tied him up, and locked him in a closet. When Judge Tyler found out the reason for their rebellion, he had no sympathy for the schoolmaster-tyrant.

In 1802, at the age of twelve, John Tyler entered the College of William and Mary in Williamsburg, Virginia, twenty-eight miles from Greenway. James Madison, called the "father of the Constitution," was president of the college at the time. Years before, Madison, Judge Tyler, and Thomas Jefferson had been college mates at William and Mary. All three were friends and "strict constructionists." They believed that the federal government had no right to take any action that was not specifically called for by the Constitution. They believed that the states had the right to make their own decisions. Young Tyler grew up with this "states' rights" view, which was widespread at the time.

Tyler showed an early interest in ancient history, law, and political science. He had visions of being a musician and became an accomplished violinist. After his graduation from William and Mary in 1807, however, he began studying law with his father. Soon it became apparent that law, not music, was to be his career.

William and Mary College in Williamsburg, Virginia

In 1809 — which marked the end of Thomas Jefferson's term as president of the United States — Tyler was admitted to the bar. He became a lawyer at the early age of nineteen. The year before, the handsome young Tyler had looked up from his studies long enough to fall in love.

Tyler's first love was the beautiful, dark-haired Letitia Christian. Born November 12, 1790, at Cedar Grove Plantation near Richmond, Virginia, Letitia was the daughter of a wealthy gentleman planter. The Christian and Tyler families had opposite political views, and Robert Christian did not want his daughter to marry the son of the Virginia governor.

18

Letitia Christian Tyler

John courted Letitia for five years. Finally, with her parents' consent, they were married on his twenty-third birthday. Many years later, one of their sons said of the long courtship: "[It] was much more formal than that of today. He was seldom alone with her before marriage, and ... never mustered up courage to kiss his sweetheart's hand until three weeks before the wedding."

Even as a young man, though spirited and headstrong, Tyler was a conservative gentleman. He had grown up in a time when there were no trains or steamboats, no telegraph—not even bicycles. All that was soon to change.

Washington, D.C., in 1800

Chapter 3

From Williamsburg
to Washington

The year 1810 found twenty-year-old John Tyler successfully practicing law. He had a gift for public speaking; it was said that he exercised great power over the feelings of an audience. Tyler was quick to find the weak points in his opponent's argument and seldom lost a case. He soon became well known throughout all of Charles City County.

In 1811, at the age of twenty-one, Tyler was elected to the Virginia legislature. This marked the beginning of his political career. Tyler became a member of the Virginia House of Delegates at the same time that General Harrison—then governor of the Indiana Territory—won the Battle of Tippecanoe. Neither man could have imagined that one day their names would be linked.

James Madison was now president of the United States, and the country was at war with Great Britain. During the War of 1812, when Virginia was threatened by British attacks, Tyler did brief military service near Richmond, serving as captain of a company of volunteers.

Above: General Harrison at the Battle of Tippecanoe, November 7, 1811
Below: Harrison at the Battle of the Thames, October 5, 1813

President James Madison

In later years, Tyler enjoyed telling about his company's stay at Williamsburg. One night the men received a false alarm that the British were coming. They had been sleeping upstairs at the college and scrambled so fast to get out that all of them, including Tyler, fell down the stairs in the dark. John Tyler, unlike Harrison, was no military hero. But as a legislator, he fully supported President Madison and the war.

Tyler grew increasingly popular in his own state. He was reelected to the Virginia House of Delegates every year for five years. Then, in 1816, he was chosen to fill a vacancy in the United States House of Representatives. At age twenty-six, John Tyler went to Washington, D.C.

The British capture and burn Washington, D.C.

The capital at the time was a ragged little town of about twelve thousand people. Its unpaved streets made travel difficult. In rainy weather, carriage wheels sank down to their hubs in mud. A large part of Washington was swampland and pasture where cows wandered about. But even in those early days it was an expensive place to live, and Tyler's family had to remain in Virginia.

The Capitol Building and the Executive Mansion (which had been burned by the British in 1814) were being rebuilt, and President Madison was living temporarily in another house. Tyler received several invitations to the Madisons' home. While he greatly admired the president and his wife, Dolley, he frowned on the French cooking Dolley had introduced recently to the capital. He wrote to Letitia that the French style with its "sauces and flumflummeries [was] intolerable." He much preferred to "dine at home in our plain way."

Above: The president's house after the fire of August 24, 1814

Right: A newspaper announcement of the peace treaty ending the War of 1812

Evening Gazette Office,

Boston, Monday, 10, a.m.

The following most highly important handbill has just been issued from the Centinel press. We deem a duty that we owe our Friends and the Public to assist in the prompt spread of the Glorious News.

Treaty of PEACE signed and arrived.

Centinel Office, Feb. 13, 1815, 8 o'clock in the morning.

WE have this instant received in Thirty-two hours from New-York the following

Great and Happy News!
FOR THE PUBLIC.

To Benjamin Russell, Esq. Centinel-Office, Boston.

New-York, Feb. 11, 1815—Saturday Evening, 10 o'clock.

SIR—

I HASTEN to acquaint you, for the information of the Public, of the arrival here this afternoon of H. Br. M. sloop of war *Favorite*, in which has come passenger Mr. Carroll, American Messenger, having in his possession

A Treaty of Peace

Between this Country and Great-Britain, signed on the 26th December last.

Mr. Baker also is on board, as Agent for the British Government, the same who was formerly Charge des Affairs here.

Mr. Carroll reached town at eight o'clock this evening. He shewed to a friend of mine, who is acquainted with him, the pacquet containing the *Treaty*, and a London newspaper of the last date of December, announcing the signing of the Treaty.

It depends, however, as my friend observed, upon the act of the President to suspend hostilities on this side.

The gentleman left London the 2d Jan. The *Transit* had sailed previously from a port on the Continent.

This city is in a perfect uproar of joy, shouts, illuminations, &c. &c.

I have undertaken to send you this by Express—the rider engaging to deliver it by Eight o'clock on Monday morning. The expense will be 225 dollars.—If you can collect so much to indemnify me I will thank you to do so.

I am with respect, Sir, your obedient servant,

JONATHAN GOODHUE.

☞ We most heartily felicitate our Country on this auspicious news, which may be relied on as wholly authentic.—Centinel.

PEACE EXTRA.

Above left: Henry Clay
Above: John C. Calhoun
Left: Daniel Webster

Tyler was impressed by the men in Congress, especially Henry Clay, John C. Calhoun, and Daniel Webster. These three would be powerful figures during Tyler's presidency, although one, Henry Clay, became a bitter enemy.

The U.S.S. *Constitution*, nicknamed "Old Ironsides," survived the War of 1812 and is now docked in Boston.

Throughout his political career, Tyler had problems earning enough money to support his growing family. Politicians were not paid well then, and serving in Congress kept him from earning a living as a lawyer. Still, Tyler voted against an increase in pay to members of Congress. His reason: "the people strongly disapprove."

During his first term as a congressman, Tyler voted in favor of funds for ships of war. He believed that a strong navy was the "most efficient means of defense" and that it was proper for the federal government to support this national defense. On the other hand, he voted against having the federal government maintain roads and canals. These "internal improvements," he felt, should be up to the individual states.

President
James
Monroe

After his first successful term in Congress, Tyler ran again and won. James Monroe was now president, and Tyler was appointed to a committee to inspect the Bank of the United States. The investigation proved to be a huge and difficult task. When it was completed, the committee members denounced the conduct of the bank and recommended that it be dissolved. Instead, the bank, which had been badly managed, was only restricted in its activities. Tyler believed that a national bank was unconstitutional. This would be one of the most heated issues he would have to face as president.

Jackson's men capture Seminole Indian chiefs in Florida.

For now, his attention was turned to Andrew Jackson. In 1817, President Monroe had ordered General Jackson to put down a Seminole Indian uprising in Florida. Jackson did so, and more. In 1818, he captured several towns in Florida and had two Englishmen executed for inciting the Indians to fight Americans. Jackson seized Pensacola, forcing its Spanish governor to flee, then brought down the Spanish flag.

Andrew Jackson leads his troops into Pensacola, Florida.

Some members of Congress wanted to vote to condemn Jackson for his handling of the Florida situation. Tyler voted along with them, agreeing that Jackson had "overstepped his orders." But Andrew Jackson was a hero to many people, and the measure did not pass.

This issue highlighted the problem of defining the government's powers. The nation was still young and struggling to form itself. The federal government did not have the authority it has today. Legislators and others heatedly debated how strictly or how loosely to interpret the Constitution. They wondered how far-reaching the powers of the federal government should be. Such questions were difficult to answer and became more complex as the nation grew.

Early settlers heading for the frontier

The great American movement across the Appalachian Mountains began during the early years of Tyler's life. On seeing the white tops of two thousand covered wagons leaving Pennsylvania, a traveler commented, "Old America seems to be breaking up and moving westward." The United States was a far different country from the one President George Washington knew only thirty years earlier. There were strong groups in the North and the South—in the industrial states and the agricultural areas—that sought to influence the federal government. The country's leaders, like Tyler, had both old and new problems to face.

SPEECH

OF

THE HONORABLE

JAMES TALLMADGE, Jr.

OF

Duchess County, New-York,

IN THE

House of Representatives of the United States,

ON

SLAVERY.

TO WHICH IS ADDED, THE PROCEEDINGS OF THE

MANUMISSION SOCIETY

OF THE CITY OF NEW-YORK,

AND THE

CORRESPONDENCE OF THEIR COMMITTEE

WITH

Messrs. Tallmadge and Taylor.

NEW-YORK:

PRINTED BY E. CONRAD,

Frankfort-street.

1819.

Reprint of a speech made during the Missouri Compromise debates

In 1819, John Tyler was unanimously reelected to the House of Representatives. In the next session of Congress, he participated in the bitter debates on whether to admit Missouri to the Union as a slave state or a free state. Tyler wrote to a friend on February 5, 1820: "Missouri is the only word ever repeated here by the politicians. You can have no possible idea of the excitement that prevails here." The North and the South were already showing dangerous signs of the Civil War that was to come.

Tyler spoke against the restrictions that the North wanted to place upon Missouri's admission to the Union. He argued that Congress had no power to restrict a new state in any way in the forming of its constitution. Missouri, which had been settled by slave owners, wanted to be admitted as a slave state. Northerners were deeply opposed to this action.

Until the Revolution, slavery had existed in all thirteen colonies. Because of the climate and the economy of the North, slavery gradually disappeared from the northern states. Many of the country's leaders, including Jefferson and Madison, had hoped that it would also disappear from the South.

Tyler, like his father, hated slavery. He worked to abolish the slave trade and believed that slavery itself would die away as it became more thinly spread out. It would be weakened by not being concentrated in the old southern states.

Tyler voted against the Missouri Compromise but, despite opposition, it passed. Though the compromise admitted Missouri as a slave state, it nevertheless prohibited slavery in the rest of the Louisiana Territory north of the 36° 30' latitude. When this vast area was settled and carved up into free states, the North would have a much more powerful voice in the federal government than would the South.

In 1821, the same year Missouri entered the Union, Tyler resigned from Congress. The long legislative battles had left him discouraged and ill. He decided not to run for reelection.

Virginia's capital city of Richmond

Tyler had been able to buy the Greenway estate, which had been sold after his father's death in 1813. Now out of public office, he gladly returned to Greenway with his wife and children.

His leisurely days did not last long, however. While at Greenway, Tyler was urged to run for a seat in the Virginia House of Delegates. He agreed, and won, embarking once again on a public career.

Two years later, in 1825, John Tyler was chosen by the Virginia legislature to be governor of Virginia. The following year he was unanimously reelected.

As governor, Tyler worked to develop and improve Virginia's schools, as his father had before him. He also

The University of Virginia at Charlottesville

strongly supported a system of canals and roads that pushed through the mountains of Virginia. Because of this system, travel and trade between the eastern and western sections of the state were no longer hampered by the mountainous countryside. Later, however, the Civil War would split Virginia into two states, now Virginia and West Virginia.

A clerk of the House of Delegates described Governor Tyler as so cordial and kind that "everybody could approach him." Tyler's popularity in his own state continued to grow. In 1827, at the age of thirty-seven, John Tyler was elected to the United States Senate. He was on his way back to Washington.

John Tyler

Chapter 4

Senator Tyler

In a letter dated December 26, 1827, Senator Tyler answered his daughter Mary's questions about the Capitol Building:

"The building is now nearly finished and is very splendid. It is so large that I have nearly lost myself in it two or three times. What principally attracts attention is the large central dome. . . ."

Tyler urged thirteen-year-old Mary to write to him frequently. "Write as you would converse," he said, "and give your mind free play."

Busy in Washington, Tyler had been unable to go home for Christmas. He attended a dinner and afterwards watched a lady and gentleman do a new dance called the waltz. It was "a dance which you have never seen," he told Mary, "and which I do not desire to see you dance. It is rather vulgar, I think."

Even more vulgar to Tyler was the mud-slinging election campaign of 1828. Andrew Jackson ran against John Quincy Adams, and the two parties told vicious stories about each other's candidates. Tyler refused to attack either candidate personally, but voted for Jackson because he was opposed to Adams's political views.

Although Tyler was a member of Jackson's Democratic-Republican party at the time, he did not fully support the man. He opposed the new president's appointment of several newspaper editors to high federal posts, marking the beginning of what was known as the spoils system.

Tyler also opposed a number of Jackson's bills for improvements of transportation facilities, such as roads, canals, and harbors. He believed that these should be state and not federal responsibilities.

Like most southerners, Tyler was against protective tariffs. These taxes on imports tended to favor the industrial North. In 1828, Congress passed what was called the "tariff of abominations," increasing tariffs on farm supplies needed by southern farmers. Greatly angered by this tariff, South Carolina threatened nullification. This meant that the state was about to declare a federal act null and void.

Tyler believed it was unconstitutional for a state to disobey the laws of the Union while enjoying the privileges of the Union. He vigorously opposed nullification but disagreed with President Jackson's strategy for handling the problem.

Jackson proposed to use military force against the nullifiers. When his "Force Bill" was put to the vote, its opponents made sure that they were absent from the House and the Senate, so that they could avoid going on record as voting against the president.

The vote was taken and the results showed thirty-two yeas and only one nay — that of Senator Tyler, who had the courage of his convictions.

An 1833 cartoon showing Calhoun defying the federal government

Tyler suggested a compromise. He helped to bring Henry Clay, a supporter of high tariffs, and John C. Calhoun, the "arch nullifier," together. Clay and Calhoun agreed on the compromise tariff of 1833, which would gradually reduce tariffs. The danger of nullification had passed at last.

In 1833, Tyler was reelected to the Senate for another six years. This time, however, his convictions did not allow him to complete his term. Ironically, the critical issue focused on the national bank.

The Bank of the United States

The Bank of the United States had changed since 1819, when Tyler served on the bank investigating committee. It was now well managed and gave stability to the national economy. Unfortunately, many people, including Jackson, disliked the bank. They felt it had too much control over the nation.

An anti-Jackson cartoon entitled "The Downfall of Mother Bank"

In 1832, Jackson denounced the bank as a monopoly, "unauthorized by the Constitution, subversive of the rights of the States, and dangerous to the liberties of the people." Jackson vetoed renewal of the bank's charter just before his overwhelming reelection to the presidency. Then, in his second term, Jackson did something that shocked everyone. He removed the government deposits from the Bank of the United States and placed them in state banks.

John Tyler had felt all along that the bank was unconstitutional. But he also believed that the president had no right to make himself the custodian of public funds. According to Tyler, Andrew Jackson had broken the law by removing the bank's deposits. In 1834, Tyler voted in favor of Clay's proposition to censure Jackson for removing the bank's funds.

In 1835, supporters of President Jackson resolved to have the censure removed from the journal of the Senate. Although the Virginia legislature had approved the censure, Jacksonians were now in control. Tyler was instructed to vote for removal of the censure. He objected as a matter of principle and honor. If he had to choose between doing what was right and maintaining his seat in Congress, his choice was clear.

Tyler told the Virginia legislature how he felt about removing the censure:

"The Constitution forbids it . . . and as an evidence of the sincerity of my convictions . . . I surrender into your hands three unexpired years of my term."

Tyler could not follow his state's instructions if it meant, in his view, violating the Constitution. He resigned as senator from Virginia in February 1836.

Tyler's refusal to vote for removal of the censure meant a complete break with the Democratic-Republican party. In 1834, the National Republicans, who were against Jackson, dropped their old name and began calling themselves Whigs. Because he could not support Jackson or Jackson's hand-picked successor, Martin Van Buren, Tyler now became a Whig.

Above: An 1837 cartoon showing Jackson riding the national bank
Below: Jackson (in stars) with his arm around Van Buren

**Martin
Van Buren**

In the election of 1836, William Henry Harrison ran for president against Van Buren and lost. Tyler was one of several candidates who ran for the office of vice-president. The president and the vice-president were elected separately in those days, and none of the vice-presidential candidates won a majority. For the first and only time in American history, the election of a vice-president was left to the Senate. They chose Richard M. Johnson, the Jackson-Van Buren favorite. Tyler was now without a public office.

A scene of Washington, D.C., from the Potomac River

John Tyler had been a hard-working and dedicated public servant. The busy senator had written to his wife, Letitia, two years earlier:

"I fear that you are really tired of looking for me, as I have been worn out with the hope ... of being able to leave here. The weather has been so mild of late that everything is once more in motion. The steamboats are upon their regular routes ... yet I am so much of a prisoner that I cannot say when I can quit the Senate chamber."

Washington, D.C., in the early 1800s

Now, sadly, the "prisoner" was free.

Tyler had earlier moved his family from Greenway to Gloucester, Virginia. Now they relocated in Williamsburg, where Tyler had a better opportunity to practice law. In 1838, however, he was again elected to the Virginia House of Delegates. The Whigs had ousted the Democratic-Republicans from control, and Tyler was honored to be made speaker of the House of Delegates.

An anti-slavery meeting on Boston Common

Tyler's political record was clear. He was a strict constructionist, believing the federal government should have limited powers. Though he disapproved of Jackson's removal of the national bank's funds, he believed the Bank of the United States itself was unconstitutional. He was against slavery, but he believed that slavery was a state issue and not a federal issue. And he was against high tariffs and internal improvements at federal expense.

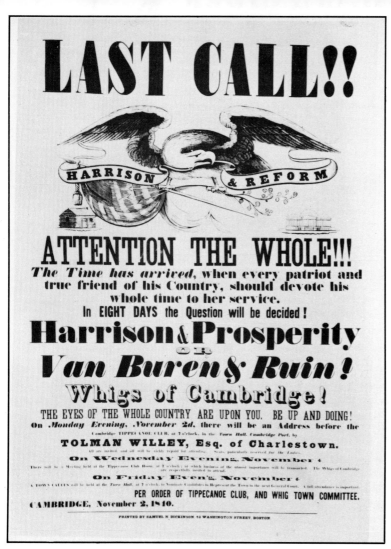

A Harrison campaign poster for the 1840 election

Most of all, John Tyler was a maverick, a man who cared less about the favor of his party than about what he believed was right. Everyone who knew him recognized this trait. Even so, in December 1839, at the Whig National Convention in Harrisburg, Pennsylvania, the party nominated John Tyler for vice-president, this time as William Henry Harrison's running mate.

When Jackson had left the White House in 1837, he was as popular as when he entered it. His successor, Martin Van Buren, was not so fortunate, however. During his

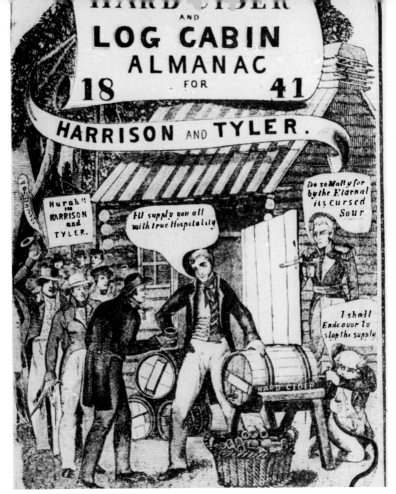

A Harrison poster showing Van Buren as a villain

administration, worldwide economic problems hurt the American economy. Farmers, businessmen, and consumers had been spending more money than they earned. Without the stability of the Bank of the United States, a panic occurred. The country sank into a deep depression that was to last for four years.

No matter what the causes of a depression, the people tend to blame the president who is in power at the time. In 1840, many people blamed Van Buren for the country's troubles. They were ready for a change.

Above: One of Harrison's "campaign barbecues" of 1840
Opposite page: Harrison-Van Buren political cartoons

The census of 1840 showed that the United States had over seventeen million people. The country was spreading westward, creating a growing class of frontier settlers and small farmers in the western territories. The Whigs used frontier folklore, western log cabins, and a great many songs to promote William Henry Harrison and Tyler— "Tippecanoe and Tyler, too"—against Van Buren in 1840.

The circus-like campaign succeeded. The victory of "Old Tippecanoe" was a Whig victory. The Whigs would soon have "Tyler, too," but as president and not as Harrison's second in command.

Standing Army,
200,000.

Laborers wan-
ted to build poor-
houses prisons &c
NB Highest wages
offered 12½ cts
per day

Sheriff sale
several farms
with cattle and
farming utensils
second hand me-
chanics tools &c

SUB TREASU
OFFICE

PRISON

MECHANICS
SHOP To Let

VAN BUREN AND RUIN.

HARRISON AND PROSPERITY.

John Tyler had a difficult time as president.
This cartoon shows him being asked to resign the presidency.

Chapter 5

The Veto President

Tyler's life was turned upside down by the death of President Harrison. At fifty-one, he was the first "accidental" president and the youngest of the nation's presidents thus far. After Harrison's death, Tyler had had to fight with his own party over whether he would be acting president or actual president. Finally, on April 14, 1841, he boldly moved into the White House as the lawful president of the country. Now he faced a Congress whose strength was massed against him by the powerful Senator Henry Clay. The cabinet that Tyler had inherited from Harrison was trying to control him. To add to the strain, his wife was very ill.

Letitia had not recovered fully since the birth of the Tylers' ninth and last child. In 1838, she had suffered a stroke. The First Lady was an almost helpless invalid when she accompanied her husband to the White House. Tyler himself had stomach problems, and the battles in which he found himself entangled did not help.

Henry Clay,
who became
John Tyler's
political enemy

Tyler had been an admirer of Henry Clay, who proved to be a forceful leader of the Whig party. As one journalist wrote of the senator from Kentucky: "He predominated over the Whig party with despotic sway. . . . Mr. Clay's wish [was] a paramount law to the whole party." Clay's obedient Whigs included almost all of Tyler's cabinet members.

Shortly after Harrison's election, Whig leaders and Harrison himself had decided that Henry Clay should be the next president. Whigs throughout the party and the Congress accepted Clay's authority. If Harrison had lived, Henry Clay might well have been the tenth president. Now Tyler was in the executive office and, unlike Harrison, he was against Clay's political views.

A portrait of Tyler by George Healy, an artist who taught himself to paint

The two men were poles apart in personality as well as in politics. Quiet and genteel, Tyler had strict rules of thought and conduct. He once wrote to his son Robert, "Half the success in life depends on manners." Clay was loud and lively. He gambled and drank and was strongly attracted to women. Americans in those days found him an exciting figure.

In the summer of 1841, President Tyler and Senator Clay had their first open clash. As the Whig leader in Congress, Clay submitted a party program to the House of Representatives. Among other things, it called for an increase in tariff rates and a rechartering of the Bank of the United States. Tyler opposed the entire program. When Congress passed Clay's bank bill, Tyler vetoed it.

The Whigs were outraged. After midnight an armed, drunken mob of them marched to the White House with drums, bugles, and guns. They shouted and hurled stones, breaking some windows. Then they burned an effigy of Tyler. Upstairs in the White House, crippled Mrs. Tyler feared for her life. The president rounded up his servants to prepare for an attack. Fortunately, after venting its rage, the crowd exhausted itself and drifted away.

Clay tried to override Tyler's veto, but could not muster enough votes. The veto was upheld. Furious, Clay prepared another bill, which Congress also passed. On September 9, 1841, true to his convictions, Tyler vetoed the second bill. When Clay had been told at a dinner party that Tyler would veto, he raged, "I will live to be a hundred years and devote them all to the extermination of Tyler and his friends!"

Henry Clay was determined to drive Tyler from office. By Saturday, September 11, all the members of Tyler's cabinet except Daniel Webster had resigned. (Webster, as secretary of state, wanted to stay in office to finish some important negotiations with England over the boundary of Maine.) If Webster had resigned, Tyler wrote, "I would necessarily have to vacate the Government by Saturday night, and . . . Whig rule would be thoroughly re-established."

Tyler was now a president without a party. The Whigs had officially expelled him. Whig newspapers called Tyler "His Accidency," and letters came to the White House from every part of the country threatening the president with assassination.

Henry Clay, a persuasive public speaker, addresses the U.S. Senate.

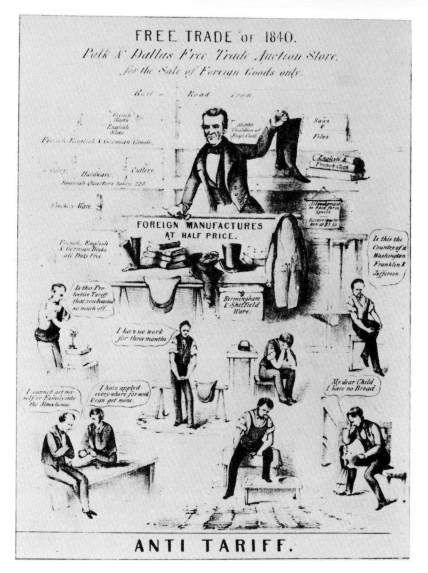

About this time, the English author Charles Dickens visited the White House. He found Tyler "pleasant . . . gentlemanly, and agreeable." However, Dickens noted, "He looked somewhat worn and anxious, and well he might be, being at war with everybody."

Tyler was not entirely alone. The president wasted no time in filling his cabinet vacancies and appointing advisers who were more in agreement with him. The business of government went on. But so did Clay's battles.

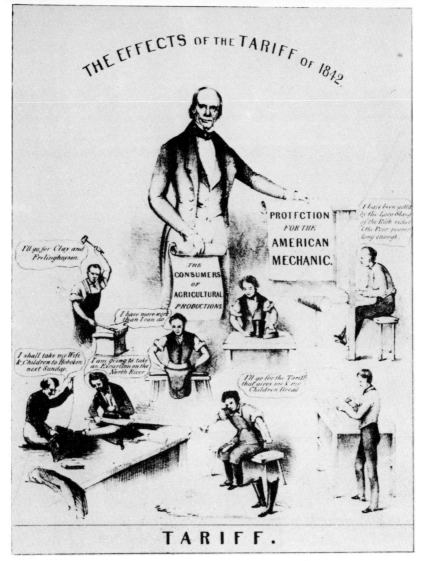

Cartoon posters about the 1842 tariff controversy—Opposite page:
James Polk offering cheap imports as American mechanics starve
Above: Henry Clay offers prosperity to American mechanics.

Clay wanted high tariffs and he wanted money from
public land sales to go to the states. Tyler opposed both
policies. He did not mind helping the debt-ridden states,
but not if it meant raising tariffs to bring in revenues for
the federal government. Higher tariffs would favor the
North and hurt the South.

An old-time stagecoach and covered wagon in the West

But Clay was determined to get the votes he needed for distribution of land sale monies to the states. People in the West were against this distribution but wanted pre-emption, or a law giving "squatters"—unofficial settlers—the right to buy their land at a low price. The East did not care about distribution or pre-emption but wanted a new national bankruptcy bill. Clay promised both sections what they wanted if they would vote for distribution. They did, and Clay's promise was kept. The Log Cabin Pre-emption Bill, which Tyler signed, became the landmark law in the settlement of the West.

Above: Burning
anti-slavery documents
in Charleston,
South Carolina

Left: This South
Carolina woman is
making hat ornaments
out of palmetto
leaves. The ornaments
were a symbol of the
state's independence.

Congress passed the distribution bill, but Tyler would not sign it. He insisted that the bill contain a provision about tariffs: distribution would stop if tariffs ever rose above the maximum of Clay's own 1833 Tariff Act.

When Clay heard of the president's sly maneuver, his anger thundered throughout the capital. The senator from Kentucky had been out-tricked—he had no choice but to agree. He weakened his distribution bill with the tariff amendment, and Tyler signed it.

As the government's financial condition grew worse, Clay and the Congressional Whigs tried to pass laws to raise tariffs without stopping distribution. Twice Tyler vetoed their bills. The Whigs cried that Tyler had no right to veto the legislation. But they should have known better. Tyler, as always, remained firm.

Only when the government desperately needed money did Tyler finally approve a raise in tariffs—adding the provision that the distribution of monies to the states had to stop.

The Whigs were beaten. They agreed to stop distribution, and Tyler signed the legislation into law. Henry Clay retired from the Senate on March 31, 1842, to prepare to be a presidential candidate in 1844.

Early in 1842, the economy was still weak. Even though it was not his fault, this made Tyler very unpopular. People even blamed him for their aches and pains. When a flu epidemic struck the nation, it was called "Tyler's Grippe." Fortunately, business began to improve in the summer months, and the country began to climb slowly out of the depression.

A convention of the Anti-Slavery Society in 1840

In July, Tyler described his busy schedule to a friend: "My course of life is to rise with the sun, and to work from that time until three o'clock. The order of despatching business pretty much is, first, all diplomatic matters; second, all matters connected with the action of Congress; third, matters of general concern falling under the executive control; then the reception of visitors, and despatch of private petitions. I dine at three-and-a-half o'clock, and in the evening my employments are miscellaneous. . . ."

Tyler's granddaughter
presides over her birthday
party at the White House.

Tyler took "some short time for exercise," and "after candle-light" received more visitors until ten at night, when he retired to bed. "So unceasing are my engagements," he wrote, that he had no time to dwell on the slanderous stories being circulated about him.

At this time, Tyler also wrote to his daughter Mary (now Mrs. Henry Jones), "Your mother's health is bad. Her mind is greatly prostrated by her disease, and she seems to be quite anxious to have you with her."

President John Tyler

Letitia Tyler died on September 10, 1842. President Tyler and his family mourned their loss.

The following January, a resolution was circulated in Congress that called for the impeachment of President Tyler. His frequent vetos of measures passed by Congress were cited as part of the reason. But the charges were not well founded, and the resolution was defeated. "Honest John" Tyler, formerly called "His Accidency," was now known as "the veto president."

Chapter 6

Accomplishments
at Home and Abroad

The 1830s and 1840s were exciting decades, bringing great changes in politics, religion, and the arts and major advances in medical science. Steamboats and railroads were replacing clipper ships and stagecoaches. The invention of cheaper printing methods made more books, magazines, and newspapers available. (And John Tyler loved to read!)

Transportation and communication were beginning to blossom during Tyler's time as well. In 1843, President Tyler signed an act that gave Samuel F. B. Morse $30,000 to connect Washington and Baltimore with his new "telegraph wire." Among the first messages that passed over the telegraph line were President Tyler's greetings from the basement of the Capitol to Chief Justice Taney, who happened to be in Baltimore. Before long, telegraph messages would be sent all over the country.

Left: Samuel F.B. Morse, inventor of the telegraph

Below: A battery-operated electrical telegraph

Above: Robert Fulton's steamship, the *Clermont*
Below: An express train on the New York and Erie Railroad line in 1840

Thomas Dorr, the leader of Rhode Island's Dorr Rebellion

These decades brought changes in the character of the nation itself. The United States had started out as a nation governed by a wealthy and educated minority. Now Americans of all classes were demanding the right to vote and to hold office. The country was moving toward greater political democracy.

In 1842, an uprising occurred in Rhode Island over the state's constitution, which allowed voting rights only to men who owned a certain amount of land. Called Dorr's Rebellion, after its leader, Thomas Dorr, this uprising was a test of the president's military powers. The governor of Rhode Island wrote to President Tyler asking for protection against violence by the rebels in his state. Tyler wished to see the dispute resolved without the use of federal military force. He handled this delicate situation skillfully and without violence. The following year Rhode Island adopted a new constitution peacefully.

One of many wandering preachers

Women also were questioning their status in the growing democracy. For centuries women had been considered inferior to men. They were not allowed to vote, to hold office, or to attend colleges or universities. They could not practice any of the professions or incorporate their own businesses. Now some women were shocking the world by demanding equal rights.

At the same time, a revivalist movement was sweeping the country. Membership in churches had fallen to a low point because of a lack of religious leaders on the frontier. Now circuit riders—dedicated ministers of all faiths— rode thousands of miles through any weather to bring religion to the wilderness. They organized camp meetings for frontier families and established new churches among the zealous pioneers.

A religious "camp meeting" around the year 1840

A different kind of politician began to be seen in Washington at this time. The frontier made for political and economic democracy, but it also made for rough manners. In the 1840s brawls became common on the House floor, and visitors to Congress could watch Representative William "Sausage" Sawyer of Ohio stuff himself with sausages on the Speaker's rostrum. Gentlemen like Tyler were becoming rare.

The United States of America was growing by leaps and bounds. But what *was* the United States? The nation's boundaries were still the subject of dispute with other countries.

John Frémont raises the flag in the Rocky Mountains in 1845.

In 1843, Tyler appointed John C. Frémont to lead an expedition to the Oregon Territory, which was jointly occupied by the United States and Great Britain. Mexico still claimed Texas and California as its own, plus what is now Nevada, Utah, Arizona, New Mexico, and parts of Wyoming and Colorado. Great Britain and the United States disagreed over the boundary lines between Canada and the United States.

In this 1842 cartoon, the United States (the Indian) offers Great Britain the choice of war or peace. Peace meant accepting the Webster-Ashburton Treaty.

The boundaries of Minnesota, New York, Vermont, New Hampshire, and Maine had never been settled. There had been outbreaks of violence along the border, with Americans helping Canadian rebels against Great Britain, and Great Britain retaliating. The situation could easily have led to another war between Britain and the United States. President Tyler knew this.

Another Webster-Ashburton cartoon. Daniel Webster is the lion.

Tyler and his secretary of state, Daniel Webster, worked together with Lord Ashburton of Great Britain to reach a compromise. There were times when Lord Ashburton did not want to continue negotiations. But finally the Webster-Ashburton Treaty of 1842 was signed, and it settled once and for all the northeastern boundary question. The northern border of the United States was finally established as far west as the Rocky Mountains. The stage was set for the coming expansion of the United States—an expansion that would take the country "from sea to shining sea."

Foreign factories along the waterfront in Canton, China

Tyler's success in foreign relations also included a treaty opening China to American trade. And Tyler again proved himself an international leader in reducing Denmark's heavy tariffs on the commerce of the world, tariffs that had originated in 1695.

Right: A Chinese woodcut showing one of the earliest European steamboats arriving in Canton with its passengers around 1840

Below: An oil painting by a Chinese artist showing foreign factories, each displaying the flag of its country

Left: Hawaii's Prince Haolilio. Right: An idol from the Sandwich Islands, brought back by a ship's captain in the 1800s

Tyler played a strong part in protecting the Sandwich Islands (later known as Hawaii). In late 1842, Prince Haolilio (or "Prince Hallelujah," as Washingtonians called him) asked Tyler for help. He believed the British and French were trying to seize his islands. Tyler sent a warning to European powers to keep away from the area, or they risked creating "dissatisfaction on the part of the United States." Through Tyler's action, the United States not only acknowledged but also protected Hawaii's independence.

Antonio López de Santa Anna

It would have surprised Tyler to learn that Hawaii was destined to be one of our fifty states. He was more concerned with California and Texas. Tyler offered to purchase California from Mexico, but his offers were rejected.

Texas had fought Mexico in 1836 to become an independent republic. But Mexican President Antonio López de Santa Anna refused to acknowledge Texan independence. Annexation of Texas to the Union, Santa Anna warned, would mean war with Mexico.

Opposite page and above: The Battle of the Alamo in Houston. There, in 1836, 183 Texan soldiers bravely battled Santa Anna's 6,000 troops until all the Americans were dead. Rallying to the cry "Remember the Alamo," Texan forces eventually defeated Santa Anna.

Britain and France had recognized Texas as a nation. The Lone Star Republic even had a navy, but it also had a huge national debt. How long could it stand alone? Tyler's dream was to annex Texas, appease Santa Anna, and eliminate British and French influence from this important area. One major problem threatened to defeat his dream: the economy of Texas depended on slavery, and Tyler could not get a two-thirds vote in the Senate for a treaty to annex a slave state.

The explosion on board the steamship *Princeton*

The Texas issue was at a standstill in the winter of 1843 when Washington society was dazzled by the arrival of Julia Gardiner, "the Rose of Long Island." This tall, dark-haired, flirtatious young woman was the daughter of New York Senator David Gardiner. President Tyler was immediately attracted to Julia, who was said to have left a string of broken hearts wherever she traveled.

In February 1844, Senator Gardiner and his daughter were guests of the president on the flagship *Princeton*. Tyler, Julia, and other guests were enjoying a buffet below when a salute was fired on the forward deck. The gun exploded as the ship passed Mount Vernon, killing Julia's father, two members of Tyler's cabinet, and five others.

Julia Gardiner Tyler

Tyler took control of the situation and ordered a rescue vessel from the Navy Yard in Washington. Julia fainted, and when the rescue vessel came alongside, Tyler carried her aboard.

Four months later John Tyler, age fifty-four, quietly married Julia Gardiner, age twenty-four. He was the first president of the United States to marry in office.

John Quincy Adams wrote in his diary: "Tyler and his bride are the laughing stock of the city."

But president-to-be James Buchanan was openly envious: "The President is the most lucky man who ever lived." Julia was not only beautiful and wealthy, she was genuinely fond of her husband, who had courted her since their first meeting.

Tyler was now in the last year of his presidency and was more determined than ever to see Texas admitted to the Union. He wanted to run for president in 1844, and Texas would add to his list of accomplishments.

Tyler had taken office when the United States was deep in a depression and had helped return the country to prosperity. He had paid off a large portion of the national debt. He had reorganized the ailing Post Office Department and brought it out of debt, reorganized and partially rebuilt the navy, and established a national weather bureau. Tyler was respected abroad for his success in foreign relations. But at home, despite his achievements, he could not muster a strong enough following to run for office. Democratic candidate James Knox Polk ran against Henry Clay and won.

Because Polk favored annexation, Tyler saw this election as proof that the people wanted Texas in the Union. He sent a message to Congress suggesting a joint House-Senate resolution to annex Texas. This would require a simple majority vote rather than the two-thirds vote in the Senate required by a treaty.

It was Tyler's last chance to bring Texas into the Union during his administration, and Julia shared his desire for immediate annexation. She made fervent speeches to senators and their wives to aid the cause. The resolution passed; and on the last day of his term, March 3, 1845, Tyler signed it.

Earlier that same year, Florida had become a state, three years after the end of the Seminole wars. Now Tyler could take the credit for adding *two* new stars to the Union flag.

Though Julia Tyler was First Lady for only eight months, she was extremely proud of her husband. During the first weeks of her marriage, her mother scolded her for spending too much time "caressing" the president instead of cleaning the "dirty" White House.

Actually, it was not Julia's fault that the White House was in a dingy, ragged condition. Congress refused to provide maintenance or improvement funds for the Executive Mansion. Tyler even had to pay for the lights and heating himself. The White House grew so shabby that an observer found its condition to be "a contemptible disgrace to the nation." Furthermore, its pillars were described as "besplattered with saliva of tobacco," its floors were covered with "patched carpets," and the "splendid draperies [were] falling in tatters."

Eventually, it was Tyler's and his wife's money that paid for repairs and renovations to the White House. Julia enjoyed her brief reign by throwing lavish parties in the new, elegant setting. It was she who first had musicians play "Hail to the Chief" as the president entered—with the First Lady on his arm.

No matter what anyone thought of John Tyler, Washingtonians flocked to his wife's almost royal entertainments. There the president and his bride actually danced the waltz he had once found so outrageous.

The grandest ball of Tyler's administration was Julia's farewell party. With over two thousand people in attendance, it was so successful that the retiring Tyler remarked, "They cannot say now that I am a President without a party!"

Chapter 7

Secession

When Tyler's term as the first "accidental" president was over, he retired to Sherwood Forest, an estate in Charles City County, three miles from the Greenway Plantation of his earlier years. There he and Julia raised his second family, five sons and two daughters.

On December 25, 1855, Tyler—then sixty-five years of age—wrote to a friend: "It is on the morning of Christmas that one realizes the happiness of having a house well filled with children."

Even in his retirement, Tyler never left politics. He continued to study national and international events. Sadly, he watched the Union moving toward Civil War.

After Abraham Lincoln's election in 1860, bitterness grew between the North and the South, and South Carolina seceded from the Union. Tyler made many speeches calling for peace. Acting as special emissary to President Buchanan in January 1861, he urged that steps be taken to avoid a war between the states. Tyler proposed that a peace convention meet in Washington, D.C. The Virginia legislature supported his idea, and delegates from several states elected Tyler president of the convention, which met in February 1861.

Julia Gardiner Tyler in her later years

From her hotel in Washington, Julia wrote to Mrs. Gardiner, her "Dear Mamma," that Tyler was "the great centre of attraction" in the capital. "Everybody says he is looked to to save the Union." But the delegates could not agree among themselves, and the resolutions Tyler finally presented to Congress were rejected. Deeply saddened, he returned to Sherwood Forest.

Tyler did not want to see the Union destroyed. He believed in the United States and its Constitution. In his judgment, however, the North had violated that Constitution, and he felt bound to support Virginia—and the South.

Tyler was a member of the Virginia convention that voted, in 1861, to secede from the Union. He was elected to the Confederate Congress and went to Richmond to attend its first session. While he was staying at the

The Tyler estate, Sherwood Forest in Virginia

Exchange Hotel in Richmond, Julia—who was traveling at the time—dreamed that he was very ill. She canceled visits to her friends to hurry to his side.

Tyler was well and surprised at Julia's unexpected arrival. But shortly after, he collapsed among friends. When he awoke, he told them, "Her dream is a true one."

John Tyler died a few days later and was buried in Hollywood Cemetery in Richmond, Virginia. Julia mourned him for the rest of her life. Twenty-seven years later, by coincidence, she died in the same hotel.

John Tyler did not live to see the devastation of the South he loved. One of our most unfairly regarded presidents, at his death he was considered a traitor to the Union. It was over fifty years later that Tyler finally received the honor due him. In 1915 Congress dedicated a monument in Hollywood Cemetery to President John Tyler.

Chronology of American History

About A.D. 982 — Eric the Red, born in Norway, reaches Greenland in one of the first European voyages to North America.

About 1000 — Leif Ericson (Eric the Red's son) leads what is thought to be the first European expedition to mainland North America; Leif probably lands in Canada.

1492 — Christopher Columbus, seeking a sea route from Spain to the Far East, discovers the New World.

1497 — John Cabot reaches Canada in the first English voyage to North America.

1513 — Ponce de Léon explores Florida in search of the fabled Fountain of Youth.

1519-1521 — Hernando Cortés of Spain conquers Mexico.

1534 — French explorers led by Jacques Cartier enter the Gulf of St. Lawrence in Canada.

1540 — Spanish explorer Francisco Coronado begins exploring the American Southwest, seeking the riches of the mythical Seven Cities of Cibola.

1565 — St. Augustine, Florida, the first permanent European town in what is now the United States, is founded by the Spanish.

1607 — Jamestown, Virginia, is founded, the first permanent English town in the present-day U.S.

1608 — Frenchman Samuel de Champlain founds the village of Quebec, Canada.

1609 — Henry Hudson explores the eastern coast of present-day U.S. for the Netherlands; the Dutch then claim parts of New York, New Jersey, Delaware, and Connecticut and name the area New Netherland.

1619 — The English colonies' first shipment of black slaves arrives in Jamestown.

1620 — English Pilgrims found Massachusetts' first permanent town at Plymouth.

1621 — Massachusetts Pilgrims and Indians hold the famous first Thanksgiving feast in colonial America.

1623 — Colonization of New Hampshire is begun by the English.

1624 — Colonization of present-day New York State is begun by the Dutch at Fort Orange (Albany).

1625 — The Dutch start building New Amsterdam (now New York City).

1630 — The town of Boston, Massachusetts, is founded by the English Puritans.

1633 — Colonization of Connecticut is begun by the English.

1634 — Colonization of Maryland is begun by the English.

1636 — Harvard, the colonies' first college, is founded in Massachusetts. Rhode Island colonization begins when Englishman Roger Williams founds Providence.

1638 — Delaware colonization begins as Swedes build Fort Christina at present-day Wilmington.

1640 — Stephen Daye of Cambridge, Massachusetts prints *The Bay Psalm Book*, the first English-language book published in what is now the U.S.

1643 — Swedish settlers begin colonizing Pennsylvania.

About 1650 — North Carolina is colonized by Virginia settlers.

1660 — New Jersey colonization is begun by the Dutch at present-day Jersey City.

1670 — South Carolina colonization is begun by the English near Charleston.

1673 — Jacques Marquette and Louis Jolliet explore the upper Mississippi River for France.

1682—Philadelphia, Pennsylvania, is settled. La Salle explores Mississippi River all the way to its mouth in Louisiana and claims the whole Mississippi Valley for France.

1693—College of William and Mary is founded in Williamsburg, Virginia.

1700—Colonial population is about 250,000.

1703—Benjamin Franklin is born in Boston.

1732—George Washington, first president of the U.S., is born in Westmoreland County, Virginia.

1733—James Oglethorpe founds Savannah, Georgia; Georgia is established as the thirteenth colony.

1735—John Adams, second president of the U.S., is born in Braintree, Massachusetts.

1737—William Byrd founds Richmond, Virginia.

1738—British troops are sent to Georgia over border dispute with Spain.

1739—Black insurrection takes place in South Carolina.

1740—English Parliament passes act allowing naturalization of immigrants to American colonies after seven-year residence.

1743—Thomas Jefferson is born in Albemarle County, Virginia. Benjamin Franklin retires at age thirty-seven to devote himself to scientific inquiries and public service.

1744—King George's War begins; France joins war effort against England.

1745—During King George's War, France raids settlements in Maine and New York.

1747—Classes begin at Princeton College in New Jersey.

1748—The Treaty of Aix-la-Chapelle concludes King George's War.

1749—Parliament legally recognizes slavery in colonies and the inauguration of the plantation system in the South. George Washington becomes the surveyor for Culpepper County in Virginia.

1750—Thomas Walker passes through and names Cumberland Gap on his way toward Kentucky region. Colonial population is about 1,200,000.

1751—James Madison, fourth president of the U.S., is born in Port Conway, Virginia. English Parliament passes Currency Act, banning New England colonies from issuing paper money. George Washington travels to Barbados.

1752—Pennsylvania Hospital, the first general hospital in the colonies, is founded in Philadelphia. Benjamin Franklin uses a kite in a thunderstorm to demonstrate that lightning is a form of electricity.

1753—George Washington delivers command that the French withdraw from the Ohio River Valley; French disregard the demand. Colonial population is about 1,328,000.

1754—French and Indian War begins (extends to Europe as the Seven Years' War). Washington surrenders at Fort Necessity.

1755—French and Indians ambush Braddock. Washington becomes commander of Virginia troops.

1756—England declares war on France.

1758—James Monroe, fifth president of the U.S., is born in Westmoreland County, Virginia.

1759—Cherokee Indian war begins in southern colonies; hostilities extend to 1761. George Washington marries Martha Dandridge Custis.

1760—George III becomes king of England. Colonial population is about 1,600,000.

1762—England declares war on Spain.

1763—Treaty of Paris concludes the French and Indian War and the Seven Years' War. England gains Canada and most other French lands east of the Mississippi River.

1764—British pass the Sugar Act to gain tax money from the colonists. The issue of taxation without representation is first introduced in Boston. John Adams marries Abigail Smith.

1765—Stamp Act goes into effect in the colonies. Business virtually stops as almost all colonists refuse to use the stamps.

1766—British repeal the Stamp Act.

1767—John Quincy Adams, sixth president of the U.S. and son of second president John Adams, is born in Braintree, Massachusetts. Andrew Jackson, seventh president of the U.S., is born in Waxhaw settlement, South Carolina.

1769—Daniel Boone sights the Kentucky Territory.

1770—In the Boston Massacre, British soldiers kill five colonists and injure six. Townshend Acts are repealed, thus eliminating all duties on imports to the colonies except tea.

1771—Benjamin Franklin begins his autobiography, a work that he will never complete. The North Carolina assembly passes the "Bloody Act," which makes rioters guilty of treason.

1772—Samuel Adams rouses colonists to consider British threats to self-government.

1773—English Parliament passes the Tea Act. Colonists dressed as Mohawk Indians board British tea ships and toss 342 casks of tea into the water in what becomes known as the Boston Tea Party. William Henry Harrison is born in Charles City County, Virginia.

1774—British close the port of Boston to punish the city for the Boston Tea Party. First Continental Congress convenes in Philadelphia.

1775—American Revolution begins with battles of Lexington and Concord, Massachusetts. Second Continental Congress opens in Philadelphia. George Washington becomes commander-in-chief of the Continental army.

1776—Declaration of Independence is adopted on July 4.

1777—Congress adopts the American flag with thirteen stars and thirteen stripes. John Adams is sent to France to negotiate peace treaty.

1778—France declares war against Great Britain and becomes U.S. ally.

1779—British surrender to Americans at Vincennes. Thomas Jefferson is elected governor of Virginia. James Madison is elected to the Continental Congress.

1780—Benedict Arnold, first American traitor, defects to the British.

1781—Articles of Confederation go into effect. Cornwallis surrenders to George Washington at Yorktown, ending the American Revolution.

1782—American commissioners, including John Adams, sign peace treaty with British in Paris. Thomas Jefferson's wife, Martha, dies. Martin Van Buren is born in Kinderhook, New York.

1784—Zachary Taylor is born near Barboursville, Virginia.

1785—Congress adopts the dollar as the unit of currency. John Adams is made minister to Great Britain. Thomas Jefferson is appointed minister to France.

1786—Shays's Rebellion begins in Massachusetts.

1787—Constitutional Convention assembles in Philadelphia, with George Washington presiding; U.S. Constitution is adopted. Delaware, New Jersey, and Pennsylvania become states.

1788—Virginia, South Carolina, New York, Connecticut, New Hampshire, Maryland, and Massachusetts become states. U.S. Constitution is ratified. New York City is declared U.S. capital.

1789—Presidential electors elect George Washington and John Adams as first president and vice-president. Thomas Jefferson is appointed secretary of state. North Carolina becomes a state. French Revolution begins.

1790—Supreme Court meets for the first time. Rhode Island becomes a state. First national census in the U.S. counts 3,929,214 persons. John Tyler is born in Charles City County, Virginia.

1791—Vermont enters the Union. U.S. Bill of Rights, the first ten amendments to the Constitution, goes into effect. District of Columbia is established. James Buchanan is born in Stony Batter, Pennsylvania.

1792—Thomas Paine publishes *The Rights of Man.* Kentucky becomes a state. Two political parties are formed in the U.S., Federalist and Republican. Washington is elected to a second term, with Adams as vice-president.

1793—War between France and Britain begins; U.S. declares neutrality. Eli Whitney invents the cotton gin; cotton production and slave labor increase in the South.

1794—Eleventh Amendment to the Constitution is passed, limiting federal courts' power. "Whiskey Rebellion" in Pennsylvania protests federal whiskey tax. James Madison marries Dolley Payne Todd.

1795—George Washington signs the Jay Treaty with Great Britain. Treaty of San Lorenzo, between U.S. and Spain, settles Florida boundary and gives U.S. right to navigate the Mississippi. James Polk is born near Pineville, North Carolina.

1796—Tennessee enters the Union. Washington gives his Farewell Address, refusing a third presidential term. John Adams is elected president and Thomas Jefferson vice-president.

1797—Adams recommends defense measures against possible war with France. Napoleon Bonaparte and his army march against Austrians in Italy. U.S. population is about 4,900,000.

1798—Washington is named commander-in-chief of the U.S. Army. Department of the Navy is created. Alien and Sedition Acts are passed. Napoleon's troops invade Egypt and Switzerland.

1799—George Washington dies at Mount Vernon, New York. James Monroe is elected governor of Virginia. French Revolution ends. Napoleon becomes ruler of France.

1800—Thomas Jefferson and Aaron Burr tie for president. U.S. capital is moved from Philadelphia to Washington, D.C. The White House is built as presidents' home. Spain returns Louisiana to France. Millard Fillmore is born in Locke, New York.

1801—After thirty-six ballots, House of Representatives elects Thomas Jefferson president, making Burr vice-president. James Madison is named secretary of state.

1802—Congress abolishes excise taxes. U.S. Military Academy is founded at West Point, New York.

1803—Ohio enters the Union. Louisiana Purchase treaty is signed with France, greatly expanding U.S. territory.

1804—Twelfth Amendment to the Constitution rules that president and vice-president be elected separately. Alexander Hamilton is killed by Vice-President Aaron Burr in a duel. Orleans Territory is established. Napoleon crowns himself emperor of France. Franklin Pierce is born in Hillsborough Lower Village, New Hampshire.

1805—Thomas Jefferson begins his second term as president. Lewis and Clark expedition reaches the Pacific Ocean.

1806—Coinage of silver dollars is stopped; resumes in 1836.

1807—Aaron Burr is acquitted in treason trial. Embargo Act closes U.S. ports to trade.

1808—James Madison is elected president. Congress outlaws importing slaves from Africa. Andrew Johnson is born in Raleigh, North Carolina.

1809—Abraham Lincoln is born near Hodgenville, Kentucky.

1810—U.S. population is 7,240,000.

1811—William Henry Harrison defeats Indians at Tippecanoe. Monroe is named secretary of state.

1812—Louisiana becomes a state. U.S. declares war on Britain (War of 1812). James Madison is reelected president. Napoleon invades Russia.

1813—British forces take Fort Niagara and Buffalo, New York.

1814—Francis Scott Key writes "The Star-Spangled Banner." British troops burn much of Washington, D.C., including the White House. Treaty of Ghent ends War of 1812. James Monroe becomes secretary of war.

1815—Napoleon meets his final defeat at Battle of Waterloo.

1816—James Monroe is elected president. Indiana becomes a state.

1817—Mississippi becomes a state. Construction on Erie Canal begins.

1818—Illinois enters the Union. The present thirteen-stripe flag is adopted. Border between U.S. and Canada is agreed upon.

1819—Alabama becomes a state. U.S. purchases Florida from Spain. Thomas Jefferson establishes the University of Virginia.

1820—James Monroe is reelected. In the Missouri Compromise, Maine enters the Union as a free (non-slave) state.

1821—Missouri enters the Union as a slave state. Santa Fe Trail opens the American Southwest. Mexico declares independence from Spain. Napoleon Bonaparte dies.

1822—U.S. recognizes Mexico and Colombia. Liberia in Africa is founded as a home for freed slaves. Ulysses S. Grant is born in Point Pleasant, Ohio. Rutherford B. Hayes is born in Delaware, Ohio.

1823—Monroe Doctrine closes North and South America to European colonizing or invasion.

1824—House of Representatives elects John Quincy Adams president when none of the four candidates wins a majority in national election. Mexico becomes a republic.

1825—Erie Canal is opened. U.S. population is 11,300,000.

1826—Thomas Jefferson and John Adams both die on July 4, the fiftieth anniversary of the Declaration of Independence.

1828—Andrew Jackson is elected president. Tariff of Abominations is passed, cutting imports.

1829—James Madison attends Virginia's constitutional convention. Slavery is abolished in Mexico. Chester A. Arthur is born in Fairfield, Vermont.

1830—Indian Removal Act to resettle Indians west of the Mississippi is approved.

1831—James Monroe dies in New York City. James A. Garfield is born in Orange, Ohio. Cyrus McCormick develops his reaper.

1832—Andrew Jackson, nominated by the new Democratic Party, is reelected president.

1833—Britain abolishes slavery in its colonies. Benjamin Harrison is born in North Bend, Ohio.

1835—Federal government becomes debt-free for the first time.

1836—Martin Van Buren becomes president. Texas wins independence from Mexico. Arkansas joins the Union. James Madison dies at Montpelier, Virginia.

1837—Michigan enters the Union. U.S. population is 15,900,000. Grover Cleveland is born in Caldwell, New Jersey.

1840—William Henry Harrison is elected president.

1841—President Harrison dies in Washington, D.C., one month after inauguration. Vice-President John Tyler succeeds him.

1843—William McKinley is born in Niles, Ohio.

1844—James Knox Polk is elected president. Samuel Morse sends first telegraphic message.

1845—Texas and Florida become states. Potato famine in Ireland causes massive emigration from Ireland to U.S. Andrew Jackson dies near Nashville, Tennessee.

1846—Iowa enters the Union. War with Mexico begins.

1847—U.S. captures Mexico City.

1848—Zachary Taylor becomes president. Treaty of Guadalupe Hidalgo ends Mexico-U.S. war. Wisconsin becomes a state.

1849—James Polk dies in Nashville, Tennessee.

1850—President Taylor dies in Washington, D.C.; Vice-President Millard Fillmore succeeds him. California enters the Union, breaking tie between slave and free states.

1852—Franklin Pierce is elected president.

1853—Gadsden Purchase transfers Mexican territory to U.S.

1854—"War for Bleeding Kansas" is fought between slave and free states.

1855—Czar Nicholas I of Russia dies, succeeded by Alexander II.

1856—James Buchanan is elected president. In Massacre of Potawatomi Creek, Kansas-slavers are murdered by free-staters. Woodrow Wilson is born in Staunton, Pennsylvania.

1857—William Howard Taft is born in Cincinnati, Ohio.

1858—Minnesota enters the Union. Theodore Roosevelt is born in New York City.

1859—Oregon becomes a state.

1860—Abraham Lincoln is elected president; South Carolina secedes from the Union in protest.

1861—Arkansas, Tennessee, North Carolina, and Virginia secede. Kansas enters the Union as a free state. Civil War begins.

1862—Union forces capture Fort Henry, Roanoke Island, Fort Donelson, Jacksonville, and New Orleans; Union armies are defeated at the battles of Bull Run and Fredericksburg. Martin Van Buren dies in Kinderhook, New York. John Tyler dies near Charles City, Virginia.

1863—Lincoln issues Emancipation Proclamation: all slaves held in rebelling territories are declared free. West Virginia becomes a state.

1864—Abraham Lincoln is reelected. Nevada becomes a state.

1865—Lincoln is assassinated in Washington, D.C., and succeeded by Andrew Johnson. U.S. Civil War ends on May 26. Thirteenth Amendment abolishes slavery. Warren G. Harding is born in Blooming Grove, Ohio.

1867—Nebraska becomes a state. U.S. buys Alaska from Russia for $7,200,000. Reconstruction Acts are passed.

1868—President Johnson is impeached for violating Tenure of Office Act, but is acquitted by Senate. Ulysses S. Grant is elected president. Fourteenth Amendment prohibits voting discrimination. James Buchanan dies in Lancaster, Pennsylvania.

1869—Franklin Pierce dies in Concord, New Hampshire.

1870—Fifteenth Amendment gives blacks the right to vote.

1872—Grant is reelected over Horace Greeley. General Amnesty Act pardons ex-Confederates. Calvin Coolidge is born in Plymouth Notch, Vermont.

1874—Millard Fillmore dies in Buffalo, New York. Herbert Hoover is born in West Branch, Iowa.

1875—Andrew Johnson dies in Carter's Station, Tennessee.

1876—Colorado enters the Union. "Custer's last stand": he and his men are massacred by Sioux Indians at Little Big Horn, Montana.

1877—Rutherford B. Hayes is elected president as all disputed votes are awarded to him.

1880—James A. Garfield is elected president.

1881—President Garfield is assassinated and dies in Elberon, New Jersey. Vice-President Chester A. Arthur succeeds him.

1882—U.S. bans Chinese immigration. Franklin D. Roosevelt is born in Hyde Park, New York.

1884—Grover Cleveland is elected president. Harry S. Truman is born in Lamar, Missouri.

1885—Ulysses S. Grant dies in Mount McGregor, New York.

1886—Statue of Liberty is dedicated. Chester A. Arthur dies in New York City.

1888—Benjamin Harrison is elected president.

1889—North Dakota, South Dakota, Washington, and Montana become states.

1890—Dwight D. Eisenhower is born in Denison, Texas. Idaho and Wyoming become states.

1892—Grover Cleveland is elected president.

1893—Rutherford B. Hayes dies in Fremont, Ohio.

1896—William McKinley is elected president. Utah becomes a state.

1898—U.S. declares war on Spain over Cuba.

1900—McKinley is reelected. Boxer Rebellion against foreigners in China begins.

1901—McKinley is assassinated by anarchist Leon Czolgosz in Buffalo, New York; Theodore Roosevelt becomes president. Benjamin Harrison dies in Indianapolis, Indiana.

1902—U.S. acquires perpetual control over Panama Canal.

1903—Alaskan frontier is settled.

1904—Russian-Japanese War breaks out. Theodore Roosevelt wins presidential election.

1905—Treaty of Portsmouth signed, ending Russian-Japanese War.

1906—U.S. troops occupy Cuba.

1907—President Roosevelt bars all Japanese immigration. Oklahoma enters the Union.

1908—William Howard Taft becomes president. Grover Cleveland dies in Princeton, New Jersey. Lyndon B. Johnson is born near Stonewall, Texas.

1909—NAACP is founded under W.E.B. DuBois

1910—China abolishes slavery.

1911—Chinese Revolution begins. Ronald Reagan is born in Tampico, Illinois.

1912—Woodrow Wilson is elected president. Arizona and New Mexico become states.

1913—Federal income tax is introduced in U.S. through the Sixteenth Amendment. Richard Nixon is born in Yorba Linda, California. Gerald Ford is born in Omaha, Nebraska.

1914—World War I begins.

1915—British liner *Lusitania* is sunk by German submarine.

1916—Wilson is reelected president.

1917—U.S. breaks diplomatic relations with Germany. Czar Nicholas of Russia abdicates as revolution begins. U.S. declares war on Austria-Hungary. John F. Kennedy is born in Brookline, Massachusetts.

1918—Wilson proclaims "Fourteen Points" as war aims. On November 11, armistice is signed between Allies and Germany.

1919—Eighteenth Amendment prohibits sale and manufacture of intoxicating liquors. Wilson presides over first League of Nations; wins Nobel Peace Prize. Theodore Roosevelt dies in Oyster Bay, New York.

1920—Nineteenth Amendment (women's suffrage) is passed. Warren Harding is elected president.

1921—Adolf Hitler's stormtroopers begin to terrorize political opponents.

1922—Irish Free State is established. Soviet states form USSR. Benito Mussolini forms Fascist government in Italy.

1923—President Harding dies in San Francisco, California; he is succeeded by Vice-President Calvin Coolidge.

1924—Coolidge is elected president. Woodrow Wilson dies in Washington, D.C. James Carter is born in Plains, Georgia. George Bush is born in Milton, Massachusetts.

1925—Hitler reorganizes Nazi Party and publishes first volume of *Mein Kampf.*

1926—Fascist youth organizations founded in Germany and Italy. Republic of Lebanon proclaimed.

1927—Stalin becomes Soviet dictator. Economic conference in Geneva attended by fifty-two nations.

1928—Herbert Hoover is elected president. U.S. and many other nations sign Kellogg-Briand pacts to outlaw war.

1929—Stock prices in New York crash on "Black Thursday"; the Great Depression begins.

1930—Bank of U.S. and its many branches close (most significant bank failure of the year). William Howard Taft dies in Washington, D.C.

1931—Emigration from U.S. exceeds immigration for first time as Depression deepens.

1932—Franklin D. Roosevelt wins presidential election in a Democratic landslide.

1933—First concentration camps are erected in Germany. U.S. recognizes USSR and resumes trade. Twenty-First Amendment repeals prohibition. Calvin Coolidge dies in Northampton, Massachusetts.

1934—Severe dust storms hit Plains states. President Roosevelt passes U.S. Social Security Act.

1936—Roosevelt is reelected. Spanish Civil War begins. Hitler and Mussolini form Rome-Berlin Axis.

1937—Roosevelt signs Neutrality Act.

1938—Roosevelt sends appeal to Hitler and Mussolini to settle European problems amicably.

1939—Germany takes over Czechoslovakia and invades Poland, starting World War II.

1940—Roosevelt is reelected for a third term.

1941—Japan bombs Pearl Harbor, U.S. declares war on Japan. Germany and Italy declare war on U.S.; U.S. then declares war on them.

1942—Allies agree not to make separate peace treaties with the enemies. U.S. government transfers more than 100,000 Nisei (Japanese-Americans) from west coast to inland concentration camps.

1943—Allied bombings of Germany begin.

1944—Roosevelt is reelected for a fourth term. Allied forces invade Normandy on D-Day.

1945—President Franklin D. Roosevelt dies in Warm Springs, Georgia; Vice-President Harry S. Truman succeeds him. Mussolini is killed; Hitler commits suicide. Germany surrenders. U.S. drops atomic bomb on Hiroshima; Japan surrenders: end of World War II.

1946—U.N. General Assembly holds its first session in London. Peace conference of twenty-one nations is held in Paris.

1947—Peace treaties are signed in Paris. "Cold War" is in full swing.

1948—U.S. passes Marshall Plan Act, providing $17 billion in aid for Europe. U.S. recognizes new nation of Israel. India and Pakistan become free of British rule. Truman is elected president.

1949—Republic of Eire is proclaimed in Dublin. Russia blocks land route access from Western Germany to Berlin; airlift begins. U.S., France, and Britain agree to merge their zones of occupation in West Germany. Apartheid program begins in South Africa.

1950—Riots in Johannesburg, South Africa, against apartheid. North Korea invades South Korea. U.N. forces land in South Korea and recapture Seoul.

1951—Twenty-Second Amendment limits president to two terms.

1952—Dwight D. Eisenhower resigns as supreme commander in Europe and is elected president.

1953—Stalin dies; struggle for power in Russia follows. Rosenbergs are executed for espionage.

1954—U.S. and Japan sign mutual defense agreement.

1955—Blacks in Montgomery, Alabama, boycott segregated bus lines.

1956—Eisenhower is reelected president. Soviet troops march into Hungary.

1957—U.S. agrees to withdraw ground forces from Japan. Russia launches first satellite, *Sputnik*.

1958—European Common Market comes into being. Fidel Castro begins war against Batista government in Cuba.

1959—Alaska becomes the forty-ninth state. Hawaii becomes fiftieth state. Castro becomes premier of Cuba. De Gaulle is proclaimed president of the Fifth Republic of France.

1960—Historic debates between Senator John F. Kennedy and Vice-President Richard Nixon are televised. Kennedy is elected president. Brezhnev becomes president of USSR.

1961—Berlin Wall is constructed. Kennedy and Khrushchev confer in Vienna. In Bay of Pigs incident, Cubans trained by CIA attempt to overthrow Castro.

1962—U.S. military council is established in South Vietnam.

1963—Riots and beatings by police and whites mark civil rights demonstrations in Birmingham, Alabama; 30,000 troops are called out, Martin Luther King, Jr., is arrested. Freedom marchers descend on Washington, D.C., to demonstrate. President Kennedy is assassinated in Dallas, Texas; Vice-President Lyndon B. Johnson is sworn in as president.

1964—U.S. aircraft bomb North Vietnam. Johnson is elected president. Herbert Hoover dies in New York City.

1965—U.S. combat troops arrive in South Vietnam.

1966—Thousands protest U.S. policy in Vietnam. National Guard quells race riots in Chicago.

1967—Six-Day War between Israel and Arab nations.

1968—Martin Luther King, Jr., is assassinated in Memphis, Tennessee. Senator Robert Kennedy is assassinated in Los Angeles. Riots and police brutality take place at Democratic National Convention in Chicago. Richard Nixon is elected president. Czechoslovakia is invaded by Soviet troops.

1969—Dwight D. Eisenhower dies in Washington, D.C. Hundreds of thousands of people in several U.S. cities demonstrate against Vietnam War.

1970—Four Vietnam War protesters are killed by National Guardsmen at Kent State University in Ohio.

1971—Twenty-Sixth Amendment allows eighteen-year-olds to vote.

1972—Nixon visits Communist China; is reelected president in near-record landslide. Watergate affair begins when five men are arrested in the Watergate hotel complex in Washington, D.C. Nixon announces resignations of aides Haldeman, Ehrlichman, and Dean and Attorney General Kleindienst as a result of Watergate-related charges. Harry S. Truman dies in Kansas City, Missouri.

1973—Vice-President Spiro Agnew resigns; Gerald Ford is named vice-president. Vietnam peace treaty is formally approved after nineteen months of negotiations. Lyndon B. Johnson dies in San Antonio, Texas.

1974—As a result of Watergate cover-up, impeachment is considered; Nixon resigns and Ford becomes president. Ford pardons Nixon and grants limited amnesty to Vietnam War draft evaders and military deserters.

1975—U.S. civilians are evacuated from Saigon, South Vietnam, as Communist forces complete takeover of South Vietnam.

1976—U.S. celebrates its Bicentennial. James Earl Carter becomes president.

1977—Carter pardons most Vietnam draft evaders, numbering some 10,000.

1980—Ronald Reagan is elected president.

1981—President Reagan is shot in the chest in assassination attempt. Sandra Day O'Connor is appointed first woman justice of the Supreme Court.

1983—U.S. troops invade island of Grenada.

1984—Reagan is reelected president. Democratic candidate Walter Mondale's running mate, Geraldine Ferraro, is the first woman selected for vice-president by a major U.S. political party.

1985—Soviet Communist Party secretary Konstantin Chernenko dies; Mikhail Gorbachev succeeds him. U.S. and Soviet officials discuss arms control in Geneva. Reagan and Gorbachev hold summit conference in Geneva. Racial tensions accelerate in South Africa.

1986—Space shuttle *Challenger* explodes shortly after takeoff; crew of seven dies. U.S. bombs bases in Libya. Corazon Aquino defeats Ferdinand Marcos in Philippine presidential election.

1987—Iraqi missile rips the U.S. frigate *Stark* in the Persian Gulf, killing thirty-seven American sailors. Congress holds hearings to investigate sale of U.S. arms to Iran to finance Nicaraguan *contra* movement.

1988—George Bush is elected president. President Reagan and Soviet leader Gorbachev sign INF treaty, eliminating intermediate nuclear forces. Severe drought sweeps the United States.

1989—East Germany opens Berlin Wall, allowing citizens free exit. Communists lose control of governments in Poland, Rumania, and Czechoslovakia. Chinese troops massacre over 1,000 pro-democracy student demonstrators in Beijing's Tiananmen Square.

Index

Page numbers in boldface type indicate illustrations.

About the Author

Dee Lillegard is the author of *September To September, Poems for All Year Round*, a teacher resource, and many easy readers, including titles for Childrens Press's *I Can Be* career series. For the *Encyclopedia of Presidents* series, she has written biographies of John Tyler, James K. Polk, James A. Garfield, and Richard Nixon. Over two hundred of Ms. Lillegard's stories, poems, and puzzles have appeared in numerous children's magazines. Ms. Lillegard lives in the San Francisco Bay Area, where she teaches Writing for Children.